# Rock-and-Roll Rabbit

Written by Rozanne Lanczak Williams
Created by Sue Lewis
Illustrated by Patty Briles

*Creative Teaching Press*

**Rock-and-Roll Rabbit**
© 2002 Creative Teaching Press, Inc.
Written by Rozanne Lanczak Williams
Illustrated by Patty Briles
Project Manager: Sue Lewis
Project Director: Carolea Williams

Published in the United States of America by:
Creative Teaching Press, Inc.
P.O. Box 2723
Huntington Beach, CA  92647-0723

CTP 3228

Rabbit can rock.

Rabbit can roll.

Rock-and-Roll Rabbit
is on the go!

Rabbit can run.

Rabbit can row.

Rock-and-Roll Rabbit
is on the go!

Rabbit can rock and row and run.

Rock-and-Roll Rabbit
is number one!

# Create your own book!

What else can Rock-and-Roll Rabbit do?
Create a list of *r* words. Then write and
illustrate a book about Rabbit.

# Words in *Rock-and-Roll Rabbit*

| Initial Consonant: *r* | High-Frequency Words | Other |
|---|---|---|
| Rabbit | can | number |
| rock | and | |
| roll | is | |
| run | on | |
| row | the | |
| Rock-and-Roll | go | |
| | one | |